CW01509035

Drama for Students, Volume 22

Project Editor: Anne Marie Hacht

Editorial: Sara Constantakis, Ira Mark Milne **Rights Acquisition and Management**: Lisa Kincade, Timothy Sisler **Manufacturing**: Rhonda Williams

Imaging: Lezlie Light, Mike Logusz, Kelly A. Quin **Product Design**: Pamela A. E. Galbreath

Product Manager: Meggin Condino

For more information, contact
Gale, an imprint of Cengage Learning
27500 Drake Rd.
Farmington Hills, MI 48331-3535
Or you can visit our Internet site at
http://www.gale.com

editors or publisher. Errors brought to the attention of the publisher and verified to the satisfaction of the publisher will be corrected in future editions.

ISBN 0-7876-8118-0
ISSN 1094-9232

Printed in the United States of America
10 9 8 7 6 5 4 3 2 1

Imaginary Friends

Nora Ephron 2002

Introduction

Lillian Hellman and Mary McCarthy had been feuding ever since they met at a writer's conference at Sarah Lawrence College in 1948. In 1980, McCarthy delivered the cruelest blow when she declared in a television interview with Dick Cavett that "every word [Lillian Hellman] writes is a lie, including 'and' and 'the.'" This comment prompted Hellman, who was watching the interview, to bring a slander suit against McCarthy. Nora Ephron's play, *Imaginary Friends*, which opened on Broadway on September 29, 2002, focuses on this lawsuit and the feuding that lead up to it.

Their bickering stemmed from, as Ephron notes in her introduction to the play, "McCarthy's love of the truth—which she turned into a religion —and... Hellman's way with a story, which she turned into a pathology." In *Imaginary Friends*, Ephron imagines a final meeting between the two women, in Hell, as they assess their lives and their antagonistic relationship through a series of razor-sharp verbal attacks on each other. Lisa D. Horowitz, in her review of the play for *Variety*, writes that Ephron's Hellman and McCarthy "prove, quite entertainingly, that they are each other's own special hell."

Author Biography

Nora Ephron was born on the Upper West Side of Manhattan on May 19, 1941 to Henry and Phoebe Ephron, prominent screenwriters of such classic films as *Daddy Long Legs*, *Desk Set*, and *Carousel*. The family moved to Beverly Hills when Nora was three years old, thus exposing her to Hollywood and setting the scene for her career in screenwriting. Ephron was raised in a family that valued verbal jousting. In an article from *Vanity Fair*, Nora's sister commented that their nightly dinner table resembled the Algonquin Round Table. Ephron's finely honed verbal skills became one of the most popular characteristics of her written work.

Ephron graduated from Wellesley College in 1962 with a degree in journalism. She used this degree to get work as an assignment reporter for *The New York Post* and as an essayist for *Esquire* and *New York* magazines. During this time, she authored three books, *Scribble, Scribble*, *Crazy Salad*, and *Wallflower at the Orgy*, that were filled with her observations of human relationships. In 1983, Ephron wrote the bestselling novel *Heartburn*, a satire of her failed marriage to Watergate journalist Carl Bernstein. *Heartburn* was later made into a film starring Meryl Streep and Jack Nicholson and won Ephron her first Academy Award Nomination.

Ephron began writing screenplays as a way to

support herself and her two sons, Jacob and Max, after her divorce. Her first screenplay *Silkwood* (1983) won an Academy Award Nomination for best original screenplay. In 1987, she married Nicholas Pileggi, journalist and screenwriter of *Goodfellas* and *Casino*. In 1989, *When Harry Met Sally*, Epron's most popular screenplay, was awarded an Academy Award for Best Script. In 1993, *Sleepless in Seattle* was released, which won Ephron another Academy Award for best script. Ephron also co-authored screenplays for the films *Michael*, *Mixed Nuts* and *You've Got Mail*.

As Ephron observed her parents and friends' screenwriting careers, which were effectively over by the time they turned 50, she decided to get involved in writing plays and directing films. Ephron began her directing career in 1992 with *This Is My Life* and her playwriting career with *Imaginary Friends*. Ephron is an active member of the Writers Guild of America, the Authors Guild, the Directors Guild of America, and the Academy of Motion Picture Arts and Sciences.

Plot Summary

Act 1

The play opens on a bare stage where two women, Lillian Hellman and Mary McCarthy, are smoking. They try to recall if they had ever met, but soon admit that they were both at Sarah Lawrence College in 1948, when the two were invited to a writers' conference there. McCarthy remembers being incensed at what she considered Hellman's lies about the Spanish civil war. She interrupted and corrected Hellman, and the two began to argue.

Hellman shifts the focus to her speech to the House Un-American Activities Committee in 1952. She recalls how she refused to identify communists by insisting, "I cannot and will not cut my conscience to fit this year's fashions," her most famous quote. The two women then bicker over details of Hellman's past and discuss other female writers. They conclude that no one reads either of them anymore.

Their conversation turns back to their personal feud, which culminated in Hellman bringing a slander suit against McCarthy for declaring in a television interview with Dick Cavett that Hellman likens their situation to a story about two U-boats who engage in battle.

The next scene jumps to Hellman's childhood

in New Orleans. Hellman plays herself as a child and reminisces about her happy experiences growing up. When she sees her father in a passionate embrace with Fizzy, a young neighbor, she falls out of the tree she had been climbing. Her nurse Sophronia comforts her and extracts a promise that she will tell no one about her father's indiscretion.

The scene changes to Minneapolis, where McCarthy and her siblings moved after her parents died. McCarthy recalls that no one actually ever told them the truth about her parents' death. They were sent to live with a great-aunt and her new husband, Uncle Myers, who physically abused her.

The action shifts to a nightclub in New York, where Hellman and McCarthy, both in their late twenties, sit drinking at the bar. In brief phrases, each begins to recant the details of her history up to that point, revealing that their lives have been remarkably similar. They begin to argue when Hellman insists that she had sex with Philip Rahv, McCarthy's lover. They each admit wanting one thing the other had, McCarthy has beauty and Hellman has wealth.

Hellman tries to compensate for her lack of beauty with the fact of her relationship with the writer Dashiell Hammett, which she romanticizes in glowing detail. McCarthy insists Hellman's vision of him is a figment of her imagination, declaring, "He was just a story." Hellman counters with the fact that Hammett gave her a true report about two schoolgirls in Scotland who accused their teachers of engaging in a lesbian relationship. She turned this story into her first play, *The Children's Hour*, which became very successful. Hellman admits that she liked the shocking nature of the play because it gained her public attention.

Literary critic and scholar Edmund Wilson comes in the bar and sits next to McCarthy, who discusses her reasons for marrying him and their subsequent stormy relationship. Philip Rahv enters when McCarthy admits that she was in love with him when she married Wilson. McCarthy and Rahv spar over class issues. After a prolonged argument, McCarthy insists that they were "incredibly happy."

McCarthy's reasons for marrying Wilson are not clear. McCarthy tells Hellman that it is odd that the two women "might never have become real writers" if they had not had relationships with older men. The two compliment each other's work. They then begin discussing their differing political positions and their activities during the cold war years, including Hellman's famous statement to the House Un-American Activities Committee.

The scene then shifts back to their meeting at Sarah Lawrence. They try to get the details straight but can agree on little. McCarthy accuses Hellman of lying about writer John Dos Passos' political activities. They continue to bicker about what happened and then wonder if they could have ever been friends. The first act ends with the appearance of Muriel Gardiner.

Act 2

The two women carry their dolls on stage and sing a song about imaginary friends to them. The scene then depicts a moment in McCarthy's past when she was beaten by her uncle. Hellman hears her screams, breaks down the door and rescues her. The two women then climb up Hellman's fig tree and hide. When Hellman announces that she has saved McCarthy, the latter gets angry, insisting that Hellman is always "trying to take over." Mary then falls out of the tree.

Two characters, Fact and Fiction, appear and sing. The scene then shifts to 1963 after the two women have become famous authors. They discuss their careers as they verbally jab at each other. After Hellman notes that she remained in the public eye while McCarthy's star faded, she becomes surrounded by interviewers asking about her childhood and especially about her story "Julia," which was made into a successful film. Hellman becomes upset when remembering the story, which she says was based on her relationship with a woman who was working for the anti-Nazi movement during World War II.

One of the reporters talks with McCarthy, telling her all the famous stories about Hellman. McCarthy starts to rehash all of the encounters the two of them have had, and includes her comment to Dick Cavett, which is all recorded by the interviewer.

The scene shifts to New York, where

McCarthy is talking to her college friend Abby Kaiser about her upcoming interview with Dick Cavett. They discuss whether or not McCarthy should use the line about Hellman being a liar that she had told to a French reporter. The two plan how she can casually insert the line so it will appear spontaneous.

In the next scene, Hellman watches McCarthy's interview with Cavett, which soon cuts to McCarthy being served with a summons. Then the action returns to New Orleans, where Hellman and McCarthy sit in the fig tree, staging Hellman's memories of her father's affair with Fizzy. When Mary takes over the scene, she has Fizzy criticize Hellman. The two women begin to fight and fall out of the tree.

In the final scene, the two women are older, looking back on the trial, noting how much publicity it got. Some of the figures involved, including lawyers and reporters, make brief appearances. McCarthy's lawyer tries to get her to retract or soften her statement about Hellman, but she refuses.

Mary calls Muriel Gardiner, a psychoanalyst, to the witness stand, who suggests that she is the real Julia that Hellman wrote about in *Pentimento*. Hellman will not admit that Julia was based on Gardiner, but claims that it does not matter one way or the other since both women became famous as a result.

Speaking as a psychoanalyst, Gardiner begins

to analyze the character of each of the two women. She determines that the lies told to Mary about her parents caused her to make "a religion out of the truth," which turned into her "blind spot." Hellman, she argues, was traumatized by seeing her father's infidelities and being told to lie about them. As a result, Hellman spent her life "telling lies and expecting to be applauded for it."

After Gardiner leaves, the two women discount her analyses and admit that the trial never took place. They argue about the motive for the lawsuit and its ultimate effect on the reputation of each. After each tries to viciously belittle the other, they attempt to leave but realize that they are "stuck together forever." They end their time on stage with a reiteration of their essential difference: McCarthy believes in the truth while Hellman believes in the story.

Muriel Gardiner

Muriel Gardiner, a psychoanalyst, is called to the imaginary witness stand in the play and suggests that she is the real Julia that Hellman wrote about in *Pentimento*. Muriel serves two purposes in the play: to support McCarthy's point that Hellman's story about her relationship with Julia is fabricated, and to psychoanalyze McCarthy and Hellman.

Dashiell Hammett

Dashiell Hammett was McCarthy's long-time companion and, she claims, lover. He appears as one of his characters, "Nick," in the film he wrote, *The Thin Man*, speaks a few lines, and then falls off a barstool, obviously drunk. By having him speak dialogue from the film, Ephron suggests that McCarthy may be right in her claim that Hellman had fabricated her account of her relationship with him.

Lillian Hellman

Ephron explains Hellman's devotion to fabrication through an examination of her past, concluding that Hellman was traumatized by seeing her father's infidelities and being told to lie about them. As a result, Gardiner insists, she spent her life "telling lies and expecting to be applauded for it." She does have a great penchant for self-promotion as she demonstrates with her stories about "Julia" and her relationship with Dashiell Hammett. At one point, during a discussion with McCarthy about top women writers, Hellman admits that she had included Jean Stafford only to make herself "seem open-minded." When a scene from McCarthy's childhood appears, in which she is being beaten by her uncle, Hellman comes to the rescue, saving her and so becoming, as she notes, the heroine of McCarthy's story. McCarthy complains that Hellman is always trying to "take over."

Hellman continually tries to heighten the drama of events even as she acknowledges that her memory is faulty. After agreeing, for example, that she told lies to the Sarah Lawrence audience, she tries to recreate the scene by putting on the bracelets that McCarthy insists she was wearing.

Although Mary McCarthy's vicious attack against Lillian Hellman's credibility was the impetus for Hellman's suit against her, which becomes the main subject of the play, Hellman appears to be nastier and more unrelenting in her jabs at McCarthy. Hellman had a reputation for cruelty, which is tempered here a bit by her wit, but still causes her to lash out repeatedly at McCarthy. Hellman obviously feels quite competitive with her foe, and perhaps her acknowledged desire to be better-looking adds fuel to her attacks, since McCarthy is an attractive woman.

Abby Kaiser

Abby Kaiser is McCarthy's college friend. Kaiser is sympathetic when McCarthy declares that her latest book is not selling well and the two women think of ways to help promote it. Abby supports McCarthy's decision to use the same line about Hellman that she told the Paris reporter, and the two discuss how to make it seem spontaneous.

Mary McCarthy

Ephron determines that McCarthy was also significantly shaped by the events of her childhood. Gardner insists that the lies told to Mary about her parents caused her to make "a religion out of the truth," which turned into her "blind spot." This blind spot caused her to overlook the consequences of her words, as she did in her famous remark about Hellman to Dick Cavett. Family, friends, and ex-lovers all tried to sue her after the publication of her essays and "fiction."

McCarthy experiences this blind spot, however, with the details of her own life as well. After an especially combative scene with her lover, Philip Rahv, McCarthy concludes, "we were incredibly happy." While she insists that she is a "a fanatic Trotskyite," she acknowledges that she became one "almost by chance," and her discussions with Rahv and Hellman suggest that she does not have strong political convictions.

As she tries to explain why she married

Edmund Wilson while she was in love with Rahv, McCarthy insists that she did not pursue him, that it just happened. Hellman points out her indecisiveness about her politics and marriage when she inquires, "what decisions in your life did you actually make?"

McCarthy also had a penchant for self-promotion as she notes that the shocking nature of her story, "The Man in the Brooks Brothers Suit," would gain her publicity. This trait became more evident as her popularity began to fade. Her remark to Cavett was spurred by her desire to promote a book that was earning her little recognition, and she eventually admits that the public feuding between the two women helped their careers.

Paris Reporter

McCarthy first declared that "every word [Hellman] writes is a lie, including 'and' and 'the,'" while speaking to a reporter. When the reporter spends most of the interview praising Hellman and the film *Julia* and has little to say about McCarthy, the latter gets angry and tries to discredit Hellman.

Philip Rahv

Philip Rahv was the editor of the *Partisan Review*, a highly-respected literary journal. He and McCarthy were lovers, and Hellman claims that she slept with him as well. He appears in one scene where he bickers with McCarthy about politics and ethnicity. McCarthy notes that he was "intense" and that they "waged class struggle[s] every day." He obviously feels he has the superior intellect and criticizes her for her "bourgeois" habits and tastes.

Themes

Ambition

Both women were extremely ambitious, which Ephron suggests was a necessary trait in the middle part of the twentieth century, when not many female authors were celebrated, let alone recognized. Both did become successful authors, but as Hellman acknowledges, they "might never have become real writers if it weren't for these two older men who came into [their] lives at almost the same moment." Hellman suggests that this was the motive for McCarthy's agreeing to marry Edmund Wilson, when she seemed to be in love with Philip Rahv.

Hellman and McCarthy understood the power of the media and used it to keep themselves in the public eye. Both women made names for themselves with their publication of shocking stories: Hellman's *The Children's Hour* and McCarthy's "The Man in the Brooks Brothers Suit." They also admit that they played up their fight for the infamy it would afford them.

In a rare moment of truth, they each confess to wanting one thing the other had, Hellman wants McCarthy's beauty and McCarthy wants Hellman's wealth. This desire was one of the impetuses for their fierce competition.

Competition

At one point McCarthy insists, "it's just too easy to say that the reason women fight with each other is because they're jealous," but jealousy was one of the factors in their ongoing battle. A more important factor, though, was their ambition. There was not a lot of room for female authors during this period, and each wanted to be considered the best.

The two women compete in every scene, over artistic success, men, and public attention. Hellman starts the battle, as McCarthy notes that she was teaching at Sarah Lawrence when Hellman came to speak by pointing out that she never "had" to teach. Hellman remembers the students never taking their eyes off of her as she told such wonderful stories. After she insists that McCarthy came to her lecture to pick a fight, she ratchets up the competition when she inquires whether it was because she slept with Rahv or if it was that McCarthy was jealous of her.

McCarthy retaliates in response to Hellman's complaint that McCarthy was always writing "mean things" about her, by admitting "I didn't write much about you." Hellman later is on the attack when she remembers watching McCarthy's interview with Cavett and declares "I was completely happy at seeing how badly you'd aged." When the two women discuss their political positions during the forties and fifties, Hellman insists that McCarthy is jealous because she and other communist sympathizers became heroes during the House Un-American Activities Committee hearings in 1952.

Their fiercest jabs are thrown when they discuss each other's work. Hellman notes that McCarthy's best-seller *The Group* was "viciously reviewed" by some of her "closest friends." McCarthy counters with her declaration that Hellman was "washed up as a playwright" and so turned to memoirs. Hellman returns by declaring that no one reads McCarthy's essays on war. At one point, they grudgingly admit that they liked each other's work, but McCarthy immediately qualifies her statement that Hellman's plays "were so well made" by claiming, "too well made, really—there was way too much of the gun over the mantel in the first act being fired at the end of the play."

Ultimately, though, they acknowledge the theatrical nature of their competition. When they identify themselves as enemies, and Hellman quotes Goethe—"you must choose your enemies well," she suggests their competition has benefited both of them.

Style

Past and Present

Ephron constantly juxtaposes present, when Hellman and McCarthy are reviewing their lives in Hell, with past, which focuses on the two women's memories. This structure helps illustrate and reinforce Ephron's focus on the tension between truth and fiction. As each character remembers details of her past, the other inevitably joins in, exclaiming, "that never happened," which is usually confirmed by both. An example of this occurs when Hellman is discussing Julia's story, which was made into a film, and which she claims was based on her own life. When Jane Fonda as Hellman in *Julia* throws her typewriter out of the window, Hellman admits that it never happened. In other scenes, Ephron has each woman editing and staging the other's memories.

Music

Ephron places songs between scenes to enhance and comment on the action of the play. Sometimes she has an ensemble, used as a traditional chorus, as in the first act when Hellman is reminiscing about her childhood. The ensemble sings "The Fig Tree Rag" to heighten the fictional nature of Hellman's memories. In the second act, Ephron introduces two male characters, Frankie

Fact and Dick Fiction, who sing about their "act." They admit that they "tend to tangle" at times, just as the main characters do, but their main point is that "fact may in fact be fiction" and "sometimes, in fact, there's fiction too."

Fascism

Fascism is a totalitarian system of government that directs the state to take absolute control of the lives of its people. The term was first used by supporters of Benito Mussolini, Italy's dictator from 1922, until his capture and execution during World War II. Other countries that have established fascistic regimes include Francisco Franco's Spain and Adolph Hitler's Germany.

Topics for Further Study

- View the film *Julia*, which depicts Hellman's relationship with Dashiell Hammett. Do you see any parallels between Ephron's Hellman and

Hellman as she is depicted in the film?

- Read Ephron's *Scribble, Scribble* and apply what she says about writing in the book to this play.

- Do a biographical study of either Hellman or McCarthy and determine whether Ephron's depiction of the two women is realistic.

- Research the terms Trotskyite and Stalinist and determine whether the play suggests that the women were true followers of these movements. Check out biographical details to see if they support Ephron's characterizations of the women in this regard.

Fascism emerged as a counter-force to the egalitarianism of socialism and democracy, which frightened many conservative Europeans at the end of the nineteenth century and the beginning of the twentieth century. They feared that the lower classes would take power away from the middle and upper classes. These conservatives also feared the chaos and general anarchy that inevitably ensue after political revolutions. Fascists played on these concerns, appealing to the people's nationalistic sentiments and promising a return to law and order and Christian morality.

The doctrine of fascism includes the glorification of the state and the complete subordination of the people to it. The state creates its own absolute law. A second principle, that of survival of the fittest, is borrowed from Social Darwinism and applied to the state. Fascists use this as a justification for aggressive imperialism, claiming that weaker countries will inevitably fall to more powerful ones. This elitist dogma extends to the fascist concept of an authoritarian leader, a superman with superior moral and intellectual powers—borrowed from the theories of philosopher Friedrich Nietzsche. This super leader would unite his people and carry on the vision of the totalitarian state.

World War II

The world experienced a decade of aggression in the 1930s that would culminate in World War II. This Second World War resulted from the rise of totalitarian regimes in Germany, Italy, and Japan. These militaristic regimes gained control as a result of the Great Depression experienced by most of the world in the early 1930s, and from the conditions created by the peace settlements following World War I. The dictatorships established in each country encouraged expansion into neighboring countries. In Germany, Hitler strengthened the army during the 1930s. In 1936, Benito Mussolini's Italian troops took Ethiopia. From 1936-39, Spain was engaged in civil war involving Francisco Franco's fascist army, aided by Germany and Italy. In March 1938,

Germany annexed Austria and in March 1939, Germany occupied Czechoslovakia. Italy took Albania in April 1939. One week after Nazi Germany and the Union of Soviet Socialist Republics (USSR) signed the Treaty of Nonaggression, on September 1, 1939, Germany invaded Poland and World War II began. On September 3, 1939, Britain and France declared war on Germany after a U-boat sank the British ship *Athenia* off the coast of Ireland. Another British ship, the *Courageous*, was sunk on September 17. All the members of the British Commonwealth, except Ireland, soon joined Britain and France in their declaration of war.

Compare & Contrast

- **1940s:** World War II comes about in response to the rise of totalitarian regimes in Germany, Italy, and Japan. Over two hundred countries band together to fight their militaristic expansion in Europe.

- **Today:** The United States, along with thirty-four other countries, invade Iraq in 2003. The initial motive for the invasion was the assumed threat of Iraq's weapons of mass destruction.

- **1940s:** The USSR emerges as a superpower.

Today: The communist system in the U.S.S.R. collapses in 1991, along with the Republic a few months later. Russia becomes increasingly more rigid under the rule of Vladimir Putin in 1999.

- **1940s:** During the years of World War II, a strong underground movement emerges that helps stop Nazi aggression through sneak attacks, sabotage, and espionage.

Today: Insurgents in Iraq, made up of Iraqi civilians and terrorist groups, carry out similar attacks against occupational forces.

The Anti-Nazi Underground Movement

During World War II an underground movement emerged in Western Europe organized by the Allies to undermine the German war machine. In France, Norway, Denmark, Holland, Belgium, Italy, and Greece, Allies created fighting forces trained in guerrilla warfare, and supported them through airdrops and radio communications from London. These resistance forces, led, for the most part, by American and British-trained officers, conducted industrial sabotage, espionage, and sneak attacks against the enemy, made and distributed propaganda, and organized escape routes for Allied prisoners of war. These activities contributed to the defeat of Germany and the end of World War II.

The Cold War

Soon after World War II, when Russian leader Joseph Stalin set up satellite communist states in Eastern Europe and Asia, the "Cold War" began, so-called because no actual fighting took place. The Cold War ushered in a new age of warfare and fear triggered by several circumstances: the United States's and the USSR's emergence as superpowers; each country's ability to use the atomic bomb; the communist expansion and the United States's determination to check it. Each side amassed stockpiles of nuclear weapons that could not only annihilate each country, but also the rest of world. Both sides declared the other the enemy and redoubled their commitment to fight for their own ideology and political and economic dominance.

As China fell to the Communists in 1949, Russia crushed the Hungarian revolution in 1956, and the United States adopted the role of world policeman, the Cold War accelerated. In 1950, the United States resolved to help South Korea repel Communist forces in North Korea. By 1953, 33,629 American soldiers had been killed in the Korean War.

The Cold War induced anxiety among Americans, who feared both annihilation by Russians and the spread of communism at home.

Americans were encouraged to stereotype all Russians as barbarians and atheists who were plotting to overthrow the US government and brainwash its citizens. The fear that communism would spread to the US led to suspicion and paranoia, and many suspected communists or communist sympathizers saw their lives ruined. This "Red Scare" was heightened by the indictments of ex-government official Alger Hiss (1950) and Julius and Ethel Rosenberg (1951) for passing defense secrets to the Russians. Soon, the United States would be engaged in a determined and often hysterical witch hunt for communists, led by Senator Joe McCarthy and the House of Representatives's Un-American Activities Committee (HUAC). (In 1954, McCarthy was censured by the Senate for his unethical behavior during the Committee sessions.) By the time of McCarthy's death in 1957, almost six million Americans had been investigated by government agencies because of their suspected Communist sympathies, yet only a few had been indicted.

Critical Overview

When *Imaginary Friends* opened on Broadway on September 29, 2002, it received both positive and negative reviews. *Time* magazine's Richard Zoglin complains that the play has "two acts full of distractions and gimmicks" and claims, "what this play needs is Roger Rewrite." Yet Lisa D. Horowitz in her review for *Variety* praises Ephron's focus and structure. She comments, "Nora Ephron's Lillian Hellman… and Mary McCarthy… prove, quite entertainingly, that they are each other's own special hell." Horowitz adds that when Ephron mixes "fact with fiction in a way that would no doubt infuriate both of her protagonists, Ephron sticks to the broad outlines of the truth while adding drama and conflict to a static situation." She applauds Ephron's use of real people, which helps "[ground] events in reality." Commenting on Ephron's inclusion of music, Horowitz determines that "the device works, adding depth and helping to avoid the monotony inherent in what is essentially a talky two-hander."

Other reviews were mixed. John Lahr, in his review for *The New Yorker*, calls the play "gleeful" and writes that it "glitters with professionalism but to almost no point." He notes McCarthy's devotion to truth and Hellman's to story and comments, "in *Imaginary Friends*, sad to say, we get neither." Most reviewers praised the subject of the play, echoing Horowitz's assessment that "Ephron makes it clear she thinks these are writers worth reading, and worth writing about.... [S]he makes them pertinent to contemporary [audiences] as well."

What Do I Read Next?

- Ephron's novel *Heartburn* (1983) chronicles the dissolution of her marriage to reporter Carl Bernstein. She later adapted the novel for the screen.

- Lillian Hellman's *Pentimento* (1973) is an autobiographical work that includes a story about a woman named Julia, a friend of Hellman's who worked for the underground during World War II.

- *Anne Frank: The Diary of a Young Girl*, published in English in 1952, chronicles the courageous life of its author, a gifted Jewish teenager, after she and her family went into hiding in Nazi-occupied Amsterdam. Anne later died in a German concentration camp.

- *Agents for Escape: Inside the French Resistance, 1939–1945* (1996) is a firsthand account of a member of the French Resistance, Andre Rougeyron. He helped downed Allied pilots return to England through an underground network of people. He was later captured and sent to the concentration camp at Buchenwald.

- Mary McCarthy's *The Group* (1963) traces the careers and relationships of a group of Vassar women from the time of their graduation until seven years later. This witty satire of American society in the 1930s follows the eight women as they struggle to live up to their ideals amid the general duplicity that surrounds them.

- McCarthy's *A Charmed Life* (1955) examines a collection of people who are defined by their historical moment.

Sources

Ephron, Nora, "Introduction," in *Imaginary Friends*, Vintage Books, 2002, pp. xi–xv.

Horowitz, Lisa D., Review of *Imaginary Friends*, in *Variety*, Vol. 388, No. 8, October 7, 2002, p. 32.

Kaufman, David, "Unfinished Women," in the *Nation*, Vol. 276, No. 3, January 27, 2003, p. 32.

Lahr, John, "Killing for Company," in the *New Yorker*, Vol. 78, No. 40, December 23, 2002, p. 163.

Zoglin, Richard, "Catfight! Broadway Resurrects a Famed Literary Spat," in *Time*, Vol. 160, No. 26, December 23, 2002.

Further Reading

Ephron, Nora, *Scribble, Scribble: Notes on the Media*, Knopf, 1978.

> Ephron collected here her hysterical columns and articles previously published in magazines like *Esquire* and *New York*.

Gelderman, Carol, ed., *Conversations with Mary McCarthy*, University Press of Mississippi, 1991.

> McCarthy discusses her life and work in a series of interviews.

Griffin, Alice, and Geraldine Thorsten, *Understanding Lillian Hellman*, Understanding Contemporary American Literature series, University of South Carolina Press, 1999.

> Griffin and Thorsten place Hellman's work into a historical context.

Grumbach, Doris, *The Company She Kept: A Revealing Portrait of Mary McCarthy*, Coward-McCann, 1967.

> Grumbach presents an intriguing account of McCarthy's life and relationships.

Hellman, Lillian, *Conversations with Lillian Hellman*, edited by Jackson Bryer, Literary Conversations series, University Press of Mississippi, 1986.

Hellman sheds light on her writing process and the themes of her plays.

Podhoretz, Norman, *Ex-Friends: Falling Out with Allen Ginsberg, Lionel & Diana Trilling, Lillian Hellman, Hannah Arendt, and Norman Mailer*, Free Press, 1999.

Podhoretz presents entertaining and insightful snapshots of Hellman's life and those of her contemporaries in the literary scene.

Rollyson, Carl, *Lillian Hellman: Her Legend and Her Legacy*, St. Martin's Press, 1998.

In an examination of newly-discovered diaries, letters, and interviews, Rollyson offers insight into Hellman's life and work.

www.ingramcontent.com/pod-product-compliance
Ingram Content Group UK Ltd.
Pitfield, Milton Keynes, MK11 3LW, UK
UKHW021559210225
4708UKWH00038B/403